One-Day Crochet: Afghans

Easy Afghan Projects You Can Complete in One Day

Barb Asselin

Asselin Group Online Publisher
R.R. #2, 449 Flat Rapids Road
Arnprior, ON Canada K7S 3G8

www.AsselinGroup.com

Copyright © 2014 Barb Asselin
First Printed June 18, 2014

All Rights reserved. No part of this book may be reproduced or used in any way or form or by any means whether electronic or mechanical, this means that you cannot record or photocopy any material ideas or text or graphics that are provided in this book.

ALSO BY BARB ASSELIN

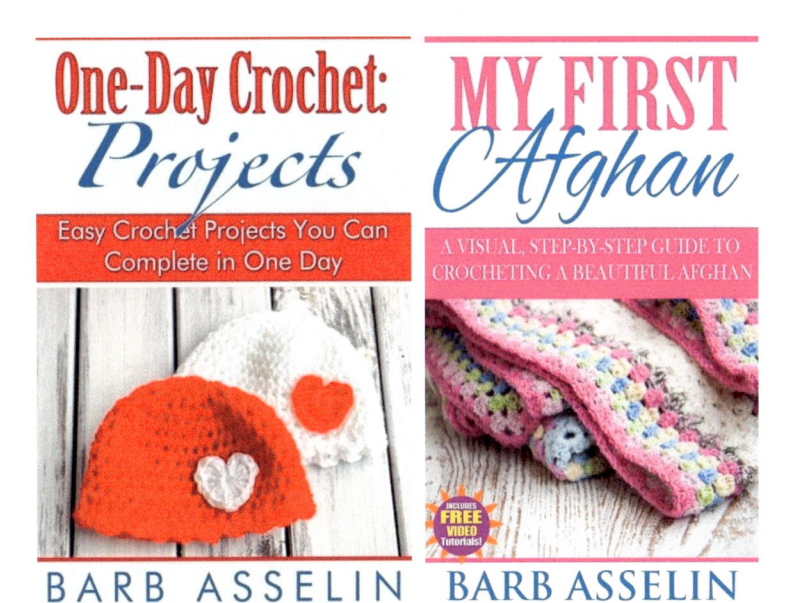

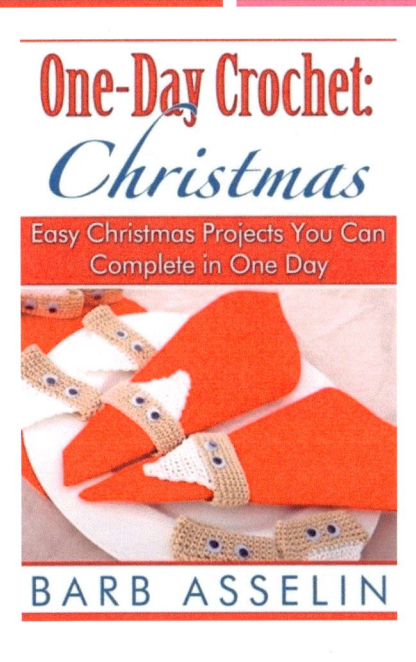

ABOUT THE AUTHOR

Barb Asselin is a college professor and best-selling author who has published books in many different genres including education, cooking, crafts, law, real estate, internet marketing, entrepreneurship, baby sign language, fitness, office administration, children's fiction and children's non-fiction.

Barb loves crafts and can often be found with her two daughters in her "craft room" finding a new project to either start or complete. She has been crocheting since her Nanny Short taught her how to chain while she was in grade school.

Since she began teaching in 2004, Barb has taught in six different programs within the School of Business and has created numerous online courses for Algonquin College including the Virtual Assistant program.

She loves to teach through her courses, books, and textbooks, and strives to make a connection with each student and reader. Barb lives in Canada with her husband, Mike, and two adorable daughters, Casey and Jamie. They enjoy music, skiing, golfing, running, and mixed martial arts.

Why You Should Read This Book

Have you always wanted to learn to crochet but thought it was too difficult?

Have you considered crocheting an afghan but thought it would take too long?

Would you like to create a special and meaningful gift for someone?

Are you looking for fun, easy and quick afghan projects to complete in just a day?

If any of these questions resound with you, then this book is for you! Inside you will find a review of the main crochet stitches and materials often used in crochet projects, in case you are new to the craft, or are looking for a refresher. Finally, you will find 10 beautiful afghan patterns that can be completed in just one day. Note that these patterns will help you complete a lap-sized blanket or a baby blanket. For larger projects, you can expect that you will need more than one day to complete.

Are you ready to be creative? Let's get started...

One-Day Crochet: Afghans
Easy Afghan Projects You Can Complete in One Day

Table of Contents

Also by Barb Asselin 3

About the Author 5

Why You Should Read This Book 7

Introduction 11

Yarn 13

    Crochet Thread 13

    Yarn Textures and Weights 13

    Types of Yarn 14

Tools 15

Standard Crochet Hook Sizes 17

Stitches 21

    Chain Stitch 21

    Slip Stitch 22

    Single Crochet 22

Double Crochet	23
Project Size Basics	25
Rainbow Afghan #1	27
Striped Afghan	31
Small Granny Square Afghan	35
Checkerboard Afghan	43
Rainbow Afghan #2	47
Giant Granny Square Afghan	53
Daisy Afghan	59
Baby Afghan #1	65
Baby Afghan #2	69
Baby Afghan #3	73
Conclusion	78
Cookbooks by Barb Asselin	79
Enjoy this book?	80

INTRODUCTION

Thank you for downloading this book and supporting an independent author. I really appreciate it. Crochet is something I have enjoyed doing since I was about 6 or 7 when my Nanny Short taught me how to make a granny square.

Knitting and crocheting are very popular in my extended family. Every year for Christmas, my Aunt Ruth used to knit my brother and me "lopi sweaters", or at least that is what we called them. They were beautiful handmade sweaters with intricate designs at the top. We also celebrated Christmas each year with handmade crocheted stockings that had Rudolph and our names on them. We still have those stockings to this day.

My Nanny Short used to make me an afghan every year, but not for Christmas. Whenever I went home (usually during the summer months), she would show up with a big garbage bag full of something and I knew that inside was another one of her beautiful creations. As I got older, the afghans got bigger. She made me single-sized afghans when I was young. When I got my first apartment, the afghans grew to double-sized. When I got married, they were queen-sized, and after I had children, they were king-sized. Plus, she made me many lap-sized afghans over the years.

Growing up in such a crafty family, you can probably guess that my spare bedroom is called the "Craft Room" and there is a closet filled to the brim with fabrics and yarn. My daughters and I love to go into the Craft Room and choose some materials and just create something new.

I hope you enjoy creating something new from this book. I specifically chose projects that would take you only one day, however, please feel free to increase the size of any of the afghans to fit your bed size, just know that it may take longer than one day. Also, please note that the "one-day" feature of this book is dependent on your experience and familiarity with crochet, the time you have available, the size of project you have chosen to make, the type of yarn you are using, and even whether or not you are multi-tasking. Each of these items can increase the time required to finish your project. If you choose a lap blanket, are familiar with all of the stitches used, use a regular weight of yarn, and are not interrupted a gazillion times, you should be able to finish your project in just one-day. If you have chosen a larger project, or are using yarn that is more challenging, or are also watching a movie at the same time, you may take longer. That's totally OK – the idea is to have fun and create a new masterpiece!

This book starts with an overview of the basic crochet stitches as well as yarn information and tools often used in crocheting. If you are a beginner at crochet or looking for a refresher, you should start here. Then, you will find 10 beautiful afghan patterns that you can create in just one day.

Enjoy!

Yarn

There are a wide variety of yarns to choose from, depending on the look of the project you are planning to make. You can choose from crochet thread, yarn of various weights and textures, as well as yarn made from various materials.

Crochet Thread

Crochet thread is used for dainty projects such as doilies, tablecloths, snowflakes, and angels. Note that the thinner the thread you use, the smaller the hook you will need.

Yarn Textures and Weights

There are a variety of weights and textures available in different types of yarns. If you are a beginner at crocheting, you should consider starting with a smooth yarn as they are the easiest to work with. Fancier yarns that are fluffier or have "eyelashes" hanging from the thread are harder to work with as it is more difficult to see the stitches as you are completing them.

The most common type of yarn for most crochet projects is worsted weight yarn. If you prefer to crochet with a heavier weight of yarn, just remember that you will need a larger size of crochet hook.

Types of Yarn

Wool Yarn

Wool yarn is a great choice if you are a beginner. You will find that it is flexible and very forgiving. If you make a mistake using wool, it is very easy to unravel that portion of your project with the mistake and re-crochet it. You may have difficulty using wool, however, if you or a family member has allergies to wool. In that case, you should choose another type of yarn. Also, wool yarn is more expensive than other types of yarn, which may be a factory for you and your project.

Cotton Yarn

Cotton yarn is less forgiving than wool yarn. It has less give to it and won't stretch. This makes it slightly harder to crochet with, especially if you are a beginner. However, it is a lighter yarn to work with, so if don't like the heat or warmth of crocheting a project made of wool, you should consider using cotton yarn.

Acrylic Yarn

Wool and cotton yarn are both natural fibers. Acrylic yarn is man-made. It is usually the least expensive option for crafters and comes in a wide variety of colors and types. It is a good choice for beginners, however, if you are looking to create a family heirloom, you may wish to choose a natural fiber.

TOOLS

    The nice thing about crochet is that you only need a hook and some yarn and you are all set to create a new project. There are a wide variety of sizes of crochet hooks available. The picture below shows a variety of fine crochet hooks that range in size. These types of metal hooks or painted metal hooks are used with thinner sizes of yarn and crochet thread.

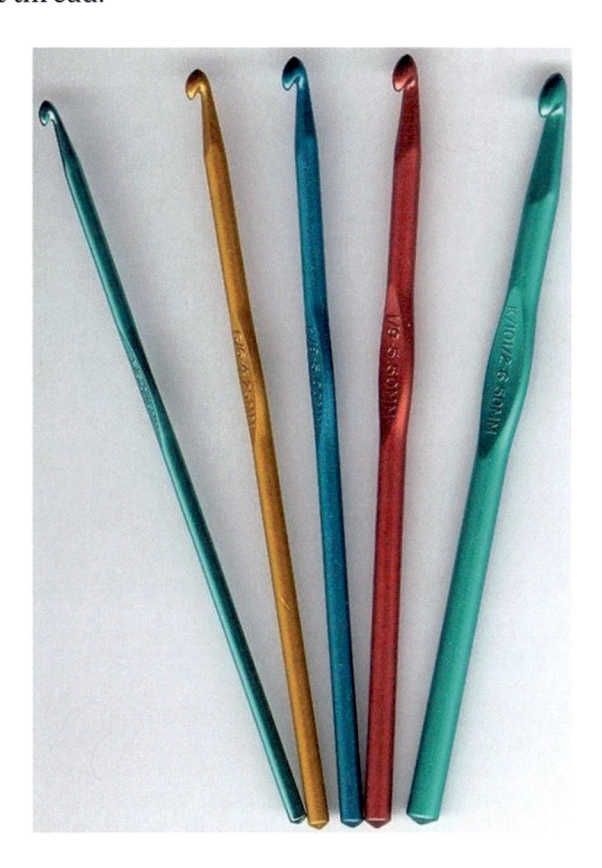

The following picture shows larger-sized crochet hooks that are made of plastic. They are used with thicker yarn and even other materials used in crochet, such as strips of fabric and novelty yarns.

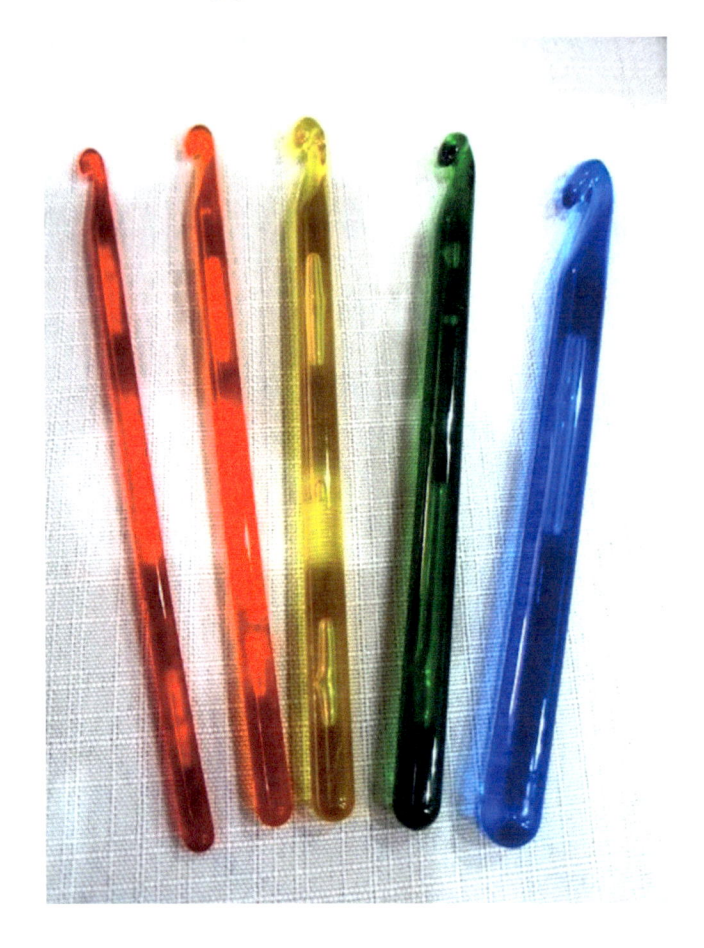

STANDARD CROCHET HOOK SIZES

It is important to use the correct size of crochet hook for the type of yarn or thread or fabric that you will be using. If you use a cotton thread and a large plastic crochet hook, your stitches will be large and loopy and your project will be very oversized and misshapen. Alternatively, it would be very difficult to crochet with thin strips of fabric using a tiny crochet hook made for cotton thread.

Once you choose a thread or yarn, the label on the outside of the yarn will indicate which size of crochet hook you should use.

Crochet hooks are sized using three methods. You will find the size on the crochet hook package as well as on the flat part in the centre of each hook. They are sized either by millimeter or by number or by letter.

The following table indicates the millimeter, letter, and number equivalencies so that you will always know which one to choose to complete your project properly.

Millimeter Range	Crochet Hook Size (Numeric)	Crochet Hook Size (Alphabetical)
2.25 mm	1	B
2.75 mm	2	C

Millimeter Range	Crochet Hook Size (Numeric)	Crochet Hook Size (Alphabetical)
3.25 mm	3	D
3.5 mm	4	E
3.75 mm	5	F
4 mm	6	G
4.5 mm	7	n/a
5 mm	8	H
5.5 mm	9	I
6 mm	10	J
6.5 mm	10.5	K
8 mm	11	L
9 mm	13	M/N
10 mm	15	N/P

Millimeter Range	Crochet Hook Size (Numeric)	Crochet Hook Size (Alphabetical)
12.75 mm	17	n/a
15 mm	19	P/Q
16 mm	n/a	Q
19 mm	35	S
25 mm	50	n/a

STITCHES

This section contains an explanation of the different types of stitches and how to make each one. There are photos for each stitch so that you can easily see if you have made it correctly.

CHAIN STITCH

Make the chain stitch (Ch) by making a slip knot or tying the yarn around your crochet hook. Loop your crochet hook under and around the yarn and use the hook to pull it through the loop on your hook. Then, loop your crochet hook under and around the yarn again and use the hook to pull it through the second loop on your hook. You will see that a chain is beginning to form. Continue until the chain is as long as your pattern requires.

Slip Stitch

The slip stitch (Sl St) is used in this book in order to join rounds or different parts of a project together. To create a slip stitch, insert your hook into the particular part of your project that is indicated in the directions. Then, loop your hook around your yarn and draw the yarn through your project.

Single Crochet

To make a single crochet (SC) insert your hook into your project. Loop the yarn over your hook and pull your hook back through your project. You will now have two loops on your crochet hook. Finally, loop the yarn around your hook and pull the yarn through both loops on your hook so that you now only have one loop on your hook.

Double Crochet

To make a double crochet (DC) loop the yarn around your hook, insert your hook into your project, loop the yarn again on your hook, and draw the yarn back through your project. Now, you will have three loops on your hook. Next, loop the yarn over your hook and pull your hook through the first two loops. Now, you will have two loops on your hook. Next, loop the yarn over your hook and pull your hook through the remaining two loops. You will now be left with one loop on your hook.

PROJECT SIZE BASICS

Now that you are familiar with the materials, tools, and stitches that will be used in your projects, let's choose a size of afghan.

Here is a list of common sizes of beds:

- Twin: 39" x 75"
- Extra long twin: 39" x 80"
- Full or double: 54" x 75"
- Queen: 60" x 80"
- King: 76" x 80"
- California king: 72" x 84"
- Crib: 28" x 52"

This is a list of common sizes of afghans:

- Children under 2 years: 24" x 30"
- Small lap blanket: 28" x 36"
- Children between 2-6: 30" x 36"
- Children between 7-11: 36" x 42"
- Children over 12: 48" x 60"
- Medium lap-sized afghan: 36" x 48"
- Adult-sized afghan: 50" x 70"

Remember that a larger-sized afghan will be more than a 1-day project, but will be very rewarding to complete. If you are looking for a true 1-day afghan project, I would suggest that you start with a baby blanket or an afghan for a child or a lap-sized afghan.

Also note that an afghan made from single crochet stitches will take much longer to crochet than an afghan made from granny squares of double or triple crochet stitches.

The afghan projects in this book will be based on creating either a baby blanket or a small lap blanket (approximately 28" x 36"). Feel free to increase the pattern in any project if you would like to create a larger sized afghan.

Some of the projects in this book will determine the amount of yarn needed by the yard or meter. For example, you may require 860 yards or 786 meters of yarn for a small lap blanket based on using worsted weight yarn and a size 5 crochet hook. If the yarn you have chosen contains 400 yards of material, you will need between 2-3 balls of yarn for that project.

Other projects will determine the amount of yarn required by the ounce. For example, if the pattern calls for 20 ounces of yarn and you are buying yarn that is sold in 5 ounce balls, you will need 4 balls of yarn for your project.

In any case, it is always a good idea to buy at least an extra 10% of yarn for your project in case your stitches are a different size than the scale used in this book.

Rainbow Afghan #1

Materials:

- Approximately 20oz. for small lap blanket or 30oz. for a medium lap blanket – 5oz. each of 6 different colors (purple, blue, green, yellow, orange, and red)
- Suggested yarn is medium weight acrylic such as Bernat Worsted
- Crochet hook size 5.00mm (H/8)
- Darning needle for weaving in ends of yarn when your project is completed
- Safety pin to temporarily mark your stitch at the beginning of your project

Gauge:

- Stitch gauge: 13 SC = 4 inches
- Row gauge: not applicable

Instructions:

Small: Ch 85

Medium: Ch 117

Start with purple

NOTE: You will change colors a lot during this project – ensure you leave a 6" tail each time for each color so that they can be woven into the project at the end

Row 1 (purple):

- Use the safety pin to temporarily mark the 1st Ch from your hook
- SC in the 3rd Ch from your hook
- Ch 1, skip the next Ch, SC in the next Ch
- Continue until you reach the end of the row
- Ch 1 and turn

Row 2 (blue):

- SC in the next Ch-1 space and then Ch 1
- Repeat this across the rest of the row
- When you reach the end of the row, SC into the stitch where you had placed your safety pin and remove the safety pin
- Ch 1 and turn

Row 3 (green):

- SC in the next Ch-1 space and then Ch 1
- Repeat this across the rest of the row

One-Day Crochet: Afghans

- When you reach the end of the row, SC into the turning Ch of the previous row
- Ch 1 and turn
- Continue until you have completed 1 SC row of each color you are using (rows 4-6)

Row 7-? (purple):

- Ch 3 and then 3-DC in the next Ch-1 space
- Ch 1 and then skip the next Ch-1 space and 3-TC in the next Ch-1 space
- Continue on in this manner until you reach the end of the row
- DC in the last stitch of the row
- Ch 3 and turn
- Continue with purple until you have a stripe that is the size you desire (or most of the yarn you have, leaving enough for 1 SC row at the end)
- Create the same number of similar DC rows with the remaining 5 colors in the same order as your SC rows in the beginning, ending with red
- In the very last row of the very last color, Ch 1 and turn

Next rows (red):

- SC in the next Ch-1 space and then Ch 1
- Continue to SC in every second stitch with Ch 1 in between each SC until the end of the row
- When you reach the end of the row, SC into the turning Ch of the previous row
- Ch 1 and turn

- Continue until you have completed 1 SC row of each color you are using (ending with purple)

Finish:

At the end, finish your last row by tying a knot in your yarn and cutting the yarn, leaving an approximately 6" tail. Use your darning needle to weave the beginning tail and the ending tail into the blanket. Use your darning needle to weave all of the tails of your project into the project from all of the color changes.

STRIPED AFGHAN

Materials:

- Approximately 20oz. for small lap blanket or 30oz. for a medium lap blanket – one-half each of two different colors
- Suggested yarn is medium weight acrylic such as Bernat Worsted
- Crochet hook size 5.00mm (H/8)
- Darning needle for weaving in ends of yarn when your project is completed
- Safety pin to temporarily mark your stitch at the beginning of your project

Gauge:

- Stitch gauge: 13 SC = 4 inches
- Row gauge: not applicable

Instructions:

Small: Ch 85

Medium: Ch 117

Row 1:

- Use the safety pin to temporarily mark the 1st Ch from your hook
- SC in the 3rd Ch from your hook
- Ch 1, skip the next Ch, SC in the next Ch
- Continue until you reach the end of the row
- Ch 1 and turn

Row 2:

- SC in the next Ch-1 space and then Ch 1
- Repeat this across the rest of the row
- When you reach the end of the row, SC into the stitch where you had placed your safety pin and remove the safety pin
- Ch 1 and turn

Row 3:

- SC in the next Ch-1 space and then Ch 1
- Repeat this across the rest of the row
- When you reach the end of the row, SC into the turning Ch of the previous row

- Ch 1 and turn
- Continue until you reach the end of your afghan
- **NOTE:** Change color after every 6 rows to create the striped effect of this project

Finish:

At the end, finish your last row by tying a knot in your yarn and cutting the yarn, leaving an approximately 6" tail. Use your darning needle to weave the beginning tail and the ending tail into the blanket.

To make the fringe on the edges of your afghan, cut 3 six-inch strands of yarn for each stitch along the side of the afghan where you will add a fringe. If you have 20 stitches, you will need 60 strands of yarn. Use 3 strands for each stitch. Hold the strands so that both ends are even. Fold all three in half, creating a loop at one end. Put your crochet hook through the first stitch and catch the loop you created. Pull the loop through the stitch so that the loop hangs below and behind the stitch. Use the hook to pull the strands of yarn through the loop, attaching it to the project. Repeat for each stitch on each side that you want a fringe. Note that the fringe will add more yarn to the requirement for this project.

SMALL GRANNY SQUARE AFGHAN

Materials:

- Approximately 20oz. for small lap blanket or 30oz. for a medium lap blanket – 4 or 5oz. each of a variety of colors, slightly heavy on the white for joining the squares together
- Suggested yarn is medium weight acrylic such as Bernat Worsted
- Crochet hook size 5.00mm (H/8)
- Darning needle for weaving in ends of yarn when your project is completed

Gauge:

- Granny squares can be worked in any gauge, just be sure to match your hook size to the recommendation on the label of the yarn you are using

Instructions:

Round 1:

- Begin with a slip knot
- Ch 6
- Join the last chain to the slip knot with a Sl St to make a circle
- Ch 3, then 2 DC, Ch 2 (all of the DC are made in the center of the circle)
- (3 DC, Ch 2) three times (all of the DC are made in the center of the circle)
- Sl St to join the last stitch made to the first stitch made to close the first round

Round 2:

- Change the color of your yarn for round 2
- Ch 3, 2 DC in Ch-2 space
- Ch 2 (this makes the corner space)
- 3 DC in the same space (this sequence makes the corner and you will do the same for every corner of your project)
- Ch 2 (this is the space you will make between crochet sections throughout each granny square)
- 3 DC in next space, Ch 2, 3 DC in same space, Ch 2

Round 1:

- Begin with a slip knot
- Ch 6
- Join the last chain to the slip knot with a Sl St to make a circle
- Ch 3, then 2 DC, Ch 2 (all of the DC are made in the center of the circle)
- (3 DC, Ch 2) three times (all of the DC are made in the center of the circle)
- Sl St to join the last stitch made to the first stitch made to close the first round

Round 2:

- Change the color of your yarn for this round
- Ch 3, 2 DC in Ch-2 space
- Ch 2 (this makes the corner space)
- 3 DC in the same space (this sequence makes the corner and you will do the same for every corner of your project)
- Ch 2 (this is the space you will make between crochet sections throughout each granny square)
- 3 DC in next space, Ch 2, 3 DC in same space, Ch 2 (this is your second corner)
- 3 DC in next space, Ch 2, 3 DC in same space, Ch 2 (this is your third corner)
- 3 DC in next space, Ch 2, 3 DC in same space, Ch 2 (this is your fourth corner)
- Sl St to join the last stitch made to the third chain stitch made in this round to close the round

Round 3:

- Change the color of your yarn for this round
- Ch 3, 2 DC in Ch-2 space
- 3 DC in next space, Ch 2, 3 DC in same space, Ch 2 (this sequence makes the corner and you will do the same for every corner of your project)
- Ch 2 (this is the space you will make between crochet sections throughout each granny square)
- 3 DC in next space (this is not a corner) and then Ch 2
- 3 DC in next space, Ch 2, 3 DC in same space (this is your second corner)
- Ch 2 and 3 DC in next space (this is not a corner) and then Ch 2
- 3 DC in next space, Ch 2, 3 DC in same space (this is your third corner)
- Ch 2 and 3 DC in next space (this is not a corner) and then Ch 2
- 3 DC in next space, Ch 2, 3 DC in same space (this is your fourth corner)
- Ch 2 and 3 DC in next space (this is not a corner) and then Ch 2
- Sl St to join the last stitch made to the third chain stitch made in this round to close the round

Round 4 and more:

- Change the color of your yarn for this round and all other rounds, ending with a round of white
- Ch 3, 2 DC in Ch-2 space
- Ch 2 and 3 DC in the next Ch-2 space (do this for all spaces until you reach the next corner)
- Ch 2

One-Day Crochet: Afghans

- 3 DC in next space, Ch 2, 3 DC in same space (this sequence makes the corner and you will do the same for every corner of your project)
- Ch 2 (this is the space you will make between crochet sections throughout each granny square)
- 3 DC in next space (this is not a corner) and then Ch 2 (do this for all spaces until you reach the next corner)
- 3 DC in next space, Ch 2, 3 DC in same space, Ch 2 (this is your second corner)
- 3 DC in next space (this is not a corner) and then Ch 2 (do this for all spaces until you reach the next corner)
- 3 DC in next space, Ch 2, 3 DC in same space, Ch 2 (this is your third corner)
- 3 DC in next space (this is not a corner) and then Ch 2 (do this for all spaces until you reach the next corner)
- 3 DC in next space, Ch 2, 3 DC in same space, Ch 2 (this is your fourth corner)
- 3 DC in next space (this is not a corner) and then Ch 2 (do this for all spaces until you reach the beginning of this round)
- Sl St to join the last stitch made to the third chain stitch made in this round to close the round

Finish:

At the end, finish your last round by tying a knot in your yarn and cutting the yarn, leaving an approximately 6" long tail. Use your darning needle to weave the beginning tail and the ending tail and all tails from changing colors into each square.

Create as many granny squares as are necessary for your project. To determine how many squares you will need, measure your finished square and divide the total dimension of your finished afghan with the size of the square to figure out how many you will need. For example, if your square is 6" wide and 6" long and you want to create an afghan that is 24" x 30", you would divide 6" into 24" and get 4 squares wide. Then, you would divide 6" into 30" and get 5 squares long. You will need 20 squares to finish your project (4 x 5). Note that your finished project may be slightly bigger as you still need to join your squares together.

You will join your squares together with white yarn. Loosely assemble your squares together on the floor or a table so that you can see how the squares will be joined together and which square will be joined with which other square or squares.

Take two squares and hold them together with the wrong sides facing outward and the right sides facing together. The project will be combined using the slip stitch (Sl St). Leave a 6" tail in your yarn before you start so that it can be woven into your project at the end. Starting at one corner of the sides to be joined, put your crochet hook through one loop on each square. Make sure you always choose the same loop on each square and each stitch. There are two loops on the outer edge of your project. You can choose either the front loop or the back loop, just be consistent throughout the joining of your project. After you have put your hook through the loops, hook it around your yarn and pull the yarn through the loops, then put your hook through the next two loops and put your joining yarn through.

Continue in this manner until the entire side has been joined together. Keep adding squares and joining sides until your entire project is complete. Finally, weave in all tails.

Checkerboard Afghan

Materials:

- Approximately 20oz. for small lap blanket or 30oz. for a medium lap blanket – half white and half a variety of colors, with black for joining the squares together
- Suggested yarn is medium weight acrylic such as Bernat Worsted
- Crochet hook size 5.00mm (H/8)
- Darning needle for weaving in ends of yarn when your project is completed

Gauge:

- Stitch gauge: 13 SC = 4 inches
- Row gauge: not applicable

Instructions:

Ch 27

NOTE: You will make half of your squares white and the other half of the squares will be a variety of colors of yarn that you have selected. The first square will be white and we will use it to measure and determine how many squares you will need for your project.

Row 1:

- Use the safety pin to temporarily mark the 1st Ch from your hook
- TC in the 3rd Ch from your hook
- Ch 1, skip the next Ch, TC in the next Ch
- Continue until you reach the end of the row
- Ch 3 and turn

Row 2:

- TC in the next Ch-3 space and then Ch 1
- Repeat this across the rest of the row
- When you reach the end of the row, TC into the stitch where you had placed your safety pin and remove the safety pin
- Ch 3 and turn

Row 3:

- TC in the next Ch-3 space and then Ch 1
- Repeat this across the rest of the row
- When you reach the end of the row, TC into the turning Ch of the previous row
- Ch 3 and turn
- Continue until your square is the length you wish it to be

Finish:

At the end, finish your last row by tying a knot in your yarn and cutting the yarn, leaving an approximately 6" long tail. Use your darning needle to weave the beginning tail and the ending tail into each square.

Create as many squares as are necessary for your project. To determine how many squares you will need, measure your finished square and divide the total dimension of your finished afghan with the size of the square to figure out how many you will need. For example, if your square is 6" wide and 6" long and you want to create an afghan that is 24" x 30", you would divide 6" into 24" and get 4 squares wide. Then, you would divide 6" into 30" and get 5 squares long. You will need 20 squares to finish your project (4 x 5). Note that your finished project may be slightly bigger as you still need to join your squares together.

Once you have determined how many squares you need, divide that number by 2. You will need this many white squares. The remaining squares will be made from different colors of yarn.

You will join your squares together with black yarn. Loosely assemble your squares together on the floor or a table so that you can see how the squares will be joined together and which square will be joined with which other square or squares.

Take two squares and hold them together with the wrong sides facing outward and the right sides facing together. The project will be combined using the single crochet (SC). Leave a 6" tail in your yarn before you start so that it can be woven into your project at the end. Starting at one corner of the sides to be joined, put your crochet hook through one loop on each square. Make sure you always choose the same loop on each square and each stitch. There are two loops on the outer edge of your project. You can choose either the front loop or the back loop, just be consistent throughout the joining of your project. First, put a slip stitch on your hook. Then, put your hook through the loops you have chosen. After you have put your hook through the loops, hook it around your yarn and pull the yarn through the loops. You will now have two loops on your hook. Now, wrap your yarn around the hook and pull it through both loops, to make a single crochet. Continue to SC to the end of the row and the entire side has been joined together. Keep adding squares and joining sides until your entire project is complete. Finally, weave in all tails.

Rainbow Afghan #2

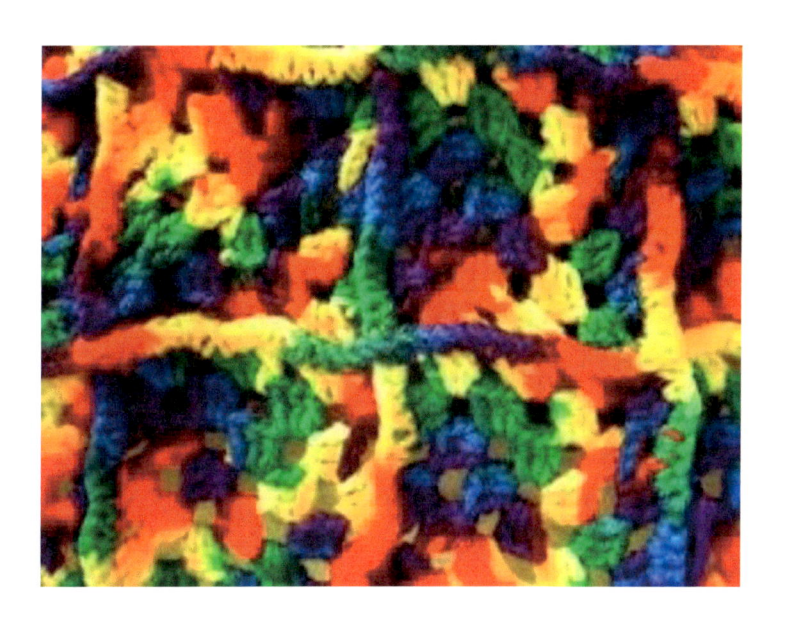

Materials:

- Approximately 20oz. for small lap blanket or 30oz. for a medium lap blanket – choose a multi-colored yarn for this project
- Suggested yarn is medium weight acrylic such as Bernat Worsted
- Crochet hook size 5.00mm (H/8)
- Darning needle for weaving in ends of yarn when your project is completed

Gauge:

- Granny squares can be worked in any gauge, just be sure to match your hook size to the recommendation on the label of the yarn you are using

Instructions:

Round 1:

- Begin with a slip knot
- Ch 6
- Join the last chain to the slip knot with a Sl St to make a circle
- Ch 3, then 2 DC, Ch 2 (all of the DC are made in the center of the circle)
- (3 DC, Ch 2) three times (all of the DC are made in the center of the circle)
- Sl St to join the last stitch made to the first stitch made to close the first round

Round 2:

- Ch 3, 2 DC in Ch-2 space
- Ch 2 (this makes the corner space)
- 3 DC in the same space (this sequence makes the corner and you will do the same for every corner of your project)
- Ch 2 (this is the space you will make between crochet sections throughout each granny square)
- 3 DC in next space, Ch 2, 3 DC in same space, Ch 2 (this is your second corner)
- 3 DC in next space, Ch 2, 3 DC in same space, Ch 2 (this is your third corner)
- 3 DC in next space, Ch 2, 3 DC in same space, Ch 2 (this is your fourth corner)
- Sl St to join the last stitch made to the third chain stitch made in this round to close the round

Round 3:

- Ch 3, 2 DC in Ch-2 space
- 3 DC in next space, Ch 2, 3 DC in same space, Ch 2 (this sequence makes the corner and you will do the same for every corner of your project)
- Ch 2 (this is the space you will make between crochet sections throughout each granny square)
- 3 DC in next space (this is not a corner) and then Ch 2
- 3 DC in next space, Ch 2, 3 DC in same space (this is your second corner)
- Ch 2 and 3 DC in next space (this is not a corner) and then Ch 2
- 3 DC in next space, Ch 2, 3 DC in same space (this is your third corner)
- Ch 2 and 3 DC in next space (this is not a corner) and then Ch 2
- 3 DC in next space, Ch 2, 3 DC in same space (this is your fourth corner)
- Ch 2 and 3 DC in next space (this is not a corner) and then Ch 2
- Sl St to join the last stitch made to the third chain stitch made in this round to close the round

Finish:

At the end, finish your third and last round by tying a knot in your yarn and cutting the yarn, leaving an approximately 6" long tail. Use your darning needle to weave the beginning tail and the ending tail and all tails into each square.

Create as many granny squares as are necessary for your project. To determine how many squares you will need, measure your finished square and divide the total dimension of your finished afghan with the size of the square to figure out how many you will need. For example, if your square is 6" wide and 6" long and you want to create an afghan that is 24" x 30", you would divide 6" into 24" and get 4 squares wide. Then, you would divide 6" into 30" and get 5 squares long. You will need 20 squares to finish your project (4 x 5). Note that your finished project may be slightly bigger as you still need to join your squares together.

You will join your squares together with the same multi-colored yarn you used for the squares. Loosely assemble your squares together on the floor or a table so that you can see how the squares will be joined together and which square will be joined with which other square or squares.

Take two squares and hold them together with the right sides facing outward and the wrong sides facing together. The project will be combined using the single crochet (SC) stitch, however, we will make the border so that it shows as a raised seam on the front side of the project. Leave a 6" tail in your yarn before you start so that it can be woven into your project at the end. Starting at one corner of the sides to be joined, put your crochet hook through both loops on each square. Make sure you always choose both loops on each square and each stitch. There are two loops on the outer edge of your project. You want to choose both the front loop and the back loop throughout the joining of your project. First, put a slip stitch on your hook. Then, put your hook through all four loops. After you have put your hook through the loops, hook it around your yarn and pull the yarn through the loops. You will now have two loops on your hook. Now, wrap your yarn around the hook and pull it through both loops, to make a single crochet. Continue to SC to the end of the row and the entire side has been joined together. Keep adding squares and joining sides until your entire project is complete. Finally, weave in all tails.

GIANT GRANNY SQUARE AFGHAN

Materials:

- Approximately 20oz. for small lap blanket or 30oz. for a medium lap blanket – approximately 40% white, 40% light blue, and 20% dark blue as in the photo, or a similar percentage of three colors of your choosing
- Suggested yarn is medium weight acrylic such as Bernat Worsted
- Crochet hook size 5.00mm (H/8)
- Darning needle for weaving in ends of yarn when your project is completed

Gauge:

- Granny squares can be worked in any gauge, just be sure to match your hook size to the recommendation on the label of the yarn you are using
- The first four rounds will be light blue, followed by two rounds of dark blue, followed by four rounds of white and then two more rounds of dark blue
- This color pattern will continue until you are finished your project

Instructions:

Round 1:

- Begin with a slip knot
- Ch 6
- Join the last chain to the slip knot with a Sl St to make a circle
- Ch 3, then 2 DC, Ch 2 (all of the DC are made in the center of the circle)
- (3 DC, Ch 2) three times (all of the DC are made in the center of the circle)
- Sl St to join the last stitch made to the first stitch made to close the first round

Round 2:

- Ch 3, 2 DC in Ch-2 space
- Ch 2 (this makes the corner space)
- 3 DC in the same space (this sequence makes the corner and you will do the same for every corner of your project)

- Ch 2 (this is the space you will make between crochet sections throughout each granny square)
- 3 DC in next space, Ch 2, 3 DC in same space, Ch 2 (this is your second corner)
- 3 DC in next space, Ch 2, 3 DC in same space, Ch 2 (this is your third corner)
- 3 DC in next space, Ch 2, 3 DC in same space, Ch 2 (this is your fourth corner)
- Sl St to join the last stitch made to the third chain stitch made in this round to close the round

Round 3:

- Ch 3, 2 DC in Ch-2 space
- 3 DC in next space, Ch 2, 3 DC in same space, Ch 2 (this sequence makes the corner and you will do the same for every corner of your project)
- Ch 2 (this is the space you will make between crochet sections throughout each granny square)
- 3 DC in next space (this is not a corner) and then Ch 2
- 3 DC in next space, Ch 2, 3 DC in same space (this is your second corner)
- Ch 2 and 3 DC in next space (this is not a corner) and then Ch 2
- 3 DC in next space, Ch 2, 3 DC in same space (this is your third corner)
- Ch 2 and 3 DC in next space (this is not a corner) and then Ch 2
- 3 DC in next space, Ch 2, 3 DC in same space (this is your fourth corner)
- Ch 2 and 3 DC in next space (this is not a corner) and then Ch 2

- Sl St to join the last stitch made to the third chain stitch made in this round to close the round

Round 4 and more:

- Ch 3, 2 DC in Ch-2 space
- Ch 2 and 3 DC in the next Ch-2 space (do this for all spaces until you reach the next corner)
- Ch 2
- 3 DC in next space, Ch 2, 3 DC in same space (this sequence makes the corner and you will do the same for every corner of your project)
- Ch 2 (this is the space you will make between crochet sections throughout each granny square)
- 3 DC in next space (this is not a corner) and then Ch 2 (do this for all spaces until you reach the next corner)
- 3 DC in next space, Ch 2, 3 DC in same space, Ch 2 (this is your second corner)
- 3 DC in next space (this is not a corner) and then Ch 2 (do this for all spaces until you reach the next corner)
- 3 DC in next space, Ch 2, 3 DC in same space, Ch 2 (this is your third corner)
- 3 DC in next space (this is not a corner) and then Ch 2 (do this for all spaces until you reach the next corner)
- 3 DC in next space, Ch 2, 3 DC in same space, Ch 2 (this is your fourth corner)
- 3 DC in next space (this is not a corner) and then Ch 2 (do this for all spaces until you reach the beginning of this round)

- Sl St to join the last stitch made to the third chain stitch made in this round to close the round
- This fourth round is the final round in your first color and then you will change color for two rounds and then use your third color for four rounds and then back to your second color for two rounds
- Continue using this color patter until you are finished

Finish:

At the end, finish your last round by tying a knot in your yarn and cutting the yarn, leaving an approximately 6" long tail. Use your darning needle to weave the beginning tail and the ending tail and all tails from changing colors into each square.

Daisy Afghan

Materials:

- Approximately 20oz. for small lap blanket or 30oz. for a medium lap blanket – approximately half of the yarn will be white with approximately 4oz. each of yellow, green, pink, and orange
- Suggested yarn is medium weight acrylic such as Bernat Worsted
- Crochet hook size 5.00mm (H/8)
- Darning needle for weaving in ends of yarn when your project is completed

Gauge:

- Granny squares can be worked in any gauge, just be sure to match your hook size to the recommendation on the label of the yarn you are using

Instructions:

Round 1 (yellow):

- Begin with a slip knot
- Ch 6
- Join the last chain to the slip knot with a Sl St to make a circle
- Ch 3, then 2 DC, Ch 2 (all of the DC are made in the center of the circle)
- (3 DC, Ch 2) three times (all of the DC are made in the center of the circle)
- Sl St to join the last stitch made to the first stitch made to close the first round

Round 2 (white):

- Change the color of your yarn for this round
- Ch 3, 2 DC in Ch-2 space
- Ch 2 (this makes the corner space)
- 3 DC in the same space (this sequence makes the corner and you will do the same for every corner of your project)
- Ch 2 (this is the space you will make between crochet sections throughout each granny square)
- 3 DC in next space, Ch 2, 3 DC in same space, Ch 2 (this is your second corner)
- 3 DC in next space, Ch 2, 3 DC in same space, Ch 2 (this is your third corner)
- 3 DC in next space, Ch 2, 3 DC in same space, Ch 2 (this is your fourth corner)
- Sl St to join the last stitch made to the third chain stitch made in this round to close the round

One-Day Crochet: Afghans

Round 3 (green):

- Change the color of your yarn for this round
- Ch 3, 2 DC in Ch-2 space
- 3 DC in next space, Ch 2, 3 DC in same space, Ch 2 (this sequence makes the corner and you will do the same for every corner of your project)
- Ch 2 (this is the space you will make between crochet sections throughout each granny square)
- 3 DC in next space (this is not a corner) and then Ch 2
- 3 DC in next space, Ch 2, 3 DC in same space (this is your second corner)
- Ch 2 and 3 DC in next space (this is not a corner) and then Ch 2
- 3 DC in next space, Ch 2, 3 DC in same space (this is your third corner)
- Ch 2 and 3 DC in next space (this is not a corner) and then Ch 2
- 3 DC in next space, Ch 2, 3 DC in same space (this is your fourth corner)
- Ch 2 and 3 DC in next space (this is not a corner) and then Ch 2
- Sl St to join the last stitch made to the third chain stitch made in this round to close the round

Round 4 and more (round 4 will be either pink or orange, followed by 2 rounds of white):

- Change the color of your yarn for this round and all other rounds, ending with two round of white
- Ch 3, 2 DC in Ch-2 space
- Ch 2 and 3 DC in the next Ch-2 space (do this for all spaces until you reach the next corner)

- Ch 2
- 3 DC in next space, Ch 2, 3 DC in same space (this sequence makes the corner and you will do the same for every corner of your project)
- Ch 2 (this is the space you will make between crochet sections throughout each granny square)
- 3 DC in next space (this is not a corner) and then Ch 2 (do this for all spaces until you reach the next corner)
- 3 DC in next space, Ch 2, 3 DC in same space, Ch 2 (this is your second corner)
- 3 DC in next space (this is not a corner) and then Ch 2 (do this for all spaces until you reach the next corner)
- 3 DC in next space, Ch 2, 3 DC in same space, Ch 2 (this is your third corner)
- 3 DC in next space (this is not a corner) and then Ch 2 (do this for all spaces until you reach the next corner)
- 3 DC in next space, Ch 2, 3 DC in same space, Ch 2 (this is your fourth corner)
- 3 DC in next space (this is not a corner) and then Ch 2 (do this for all spaces until you reach the beginning of this round)
- Sl St to join the last stitch made to the third chain stitch made in this round to close the round

Finish:

At the end, finish your last round by tying a knot in your yarn and cutting the yarn, leaving an approximately 6" long tail. Use your darning needle to weave the beginning tail

One-Day Crochet: Afghans

and the ending tail and all tails from changing colors into each square.

Create as many granny squares as are necessary for your project. To determine how many squares you will need, measure your finished square and divide the total dimension of your finished afghan with the size of the square to figure out how many you will need. For example, if your square is 6" wide and 6" long and you want to create an afghan that is 24" x 30", you would divide 6" into 24" and get 4 squares wide. Then, you would divide 6" into 30" and get 5 squares long. You will need 20 squares to finish your project (4 x 5). Note that your finished project may be slightly bigger as you still need to join your squares together.

You will join your squares together with white yarn. Loosely assemble your squares together on the floor or a table so that you can see how the squares will be joined together and which square will be joined with which other square or squares.

Take two squares and hold them together with the wrong sides facing outward and the right sides facing together. The project will be combined using the slip stitch (Sl St). Leave a 6" tail in your yarn before you start so that it can be woven into your project at the end. Starting at one corner of the sides to be joined, put your crochet hook through one loop on each square. Make sure you always choose the same loop on each square and each stitch. There are two loops on the outer edge of your project. You can choose either the front loop or the back loop, just be consistent throughout the joining of your project. After you have put your hook through the loops, hook it around your yarn and pull the yarn through the loops, then put your hook through the next two loops and put your joining yarn through. Continue in this manner until the entire side has been joined together. Keep adding squares and joining sides until your entire project is complete. Finally, weave in all tails.

Baby Afghan #1

Materials:

- Approximately 10oz. of yarn for small, 15oz. for medium, or 20oz. for large-sized baby blanket (half light pink and half light blue)
- Suggested yarn is 5oz. light weight acrylic such as Bernat Softee
- Crochet hook size 4.00mm (G/6)
- Darning needle for weaving in ends of yarn when your project is completed

Gauge:

- Stitch gauge: 4 stitches = 1 inch
- Row gauge: not applicable

Instructions (start with light pink):

Small: Ch 105

Medium: Ch 121

Large: Ch 145

NOTE: You will change colors a lot during this project – ensure you leave a 6" tail each time for each color so that they can be woven into the project at the end

Row 1 (light pink):

- DC in the 3rd Ch from your hook
- Ch 1, skip the next Ch, 3-DC in the next Ch
- Continue until you reach the end of the row
- Ch 3 and then 3-DC in the next Ch-1 space
- Ch 1 and then skip the next Ch-1 space and 3-DC in the next Ch-1 space
- Continue on in this manner until you reach the end of the row
- DC in the last stitch of the row
- Ch 3 and turn

Row 2 (light pink):

- 3-DC in the next Ch-1 space
- Ch 1 and then 3-DC in the next Ch-1 space
- Continue on in this manner until you reach the end of the row
- DC in the last stitch of the row
- Ch 3 and turn

Row 3 (light blue):

- 3-DC in the next Ch-1 space
- Ch 1 and then 3-DC in the next Ch-1 space
- Continue on in this manner until you reach the end of the row
- DC in the last stitch of the row
- Ch 3 and turn
- Continue until you have completed your afghan, alternating between two rows of light pink and two rows of light blue

Finish:

At the end, finish your last row by tying a knot in your yarn and cutting the yarn, leaving an approximately 6" tail. Use your darning needle to weave the beginning tail and the ending tail into the blanket. Use your darning needle to weave all of the tails of your project into the project from all of the color changes.

To make the fringe on the edges of your afghan, cut 3 12-inch strands of yarn for each stitch along the side of the afghan where you will add a fringe. If you have 20 stitches, you will need 120 strands of yarn. Use 3 strands for each stitch. Hold the strands so that both ends are even. Fold all three in half, creating a loop at one end. Put your crochet hook through the first stitch and catch the loop you created. Pull the loop through the stitch so that the loop hangs below and behind the stitch. Use the hook to pull the strands of yarn through the loop, attaching it to the project. Repeat for each stitch on each side that you want a fringe. Note that the fringe will add more yarn to the requirement for this project.

Baby Afghan #2

Materials:

- Approximately 10oz. of yarn for small, 15oz. for medium, or 20oz. for large-sized baby blanket
- Suggested yarn is 5oz. light weight acrylic such as Bernat Softee
- Crochet hook size 4.00mm (G/6)
- Darning needle for weaving in ends of yarn when your project is completed
- Safety pin to temporarily mark your stitch at the beginning of your project

Gauge:

- Stitch gauge: 4 stitches = 1 inch
- Row gauge: not applicable

Instructions:

Small: Ch 105

Medium: Ch 121

Large: Ch 145

Row 1:

- Use the safety pin to temporarily mark the 1st Ch from your hook
- SC in the 3rd Ch from your hook
- Ch 1, skip the next Ch, SC in the next Ch
- Continue until you reach the end of the row
- Ch 1 and turn

Row 2:

- SC in the next Ch-1 space and then Ch 1
- Repeat this across the rest of the row
- When you reach the end of the row, SC into the stitch where you had placed your safety pin and remove the safety pin
- Ch 1 and turn

Row 3:

- SC in the next Ch-1 space and then Ch 1
- Repeat this across the rest of the row

- When you reach the end of the row, SC into the turning Ch of the previous row
- Ch 1 and turn
- Continue until you reach the end of your afghan

Finish:

At the end, finish your last row by tying a knot in your yarn and cutting the yarn, leaving an approximately 6" tail. Use your darning needle to weave the beginning tail and the ending tail into the blanket.

One-Day Crochet: Afghans   73

BABY AFGHAN #3

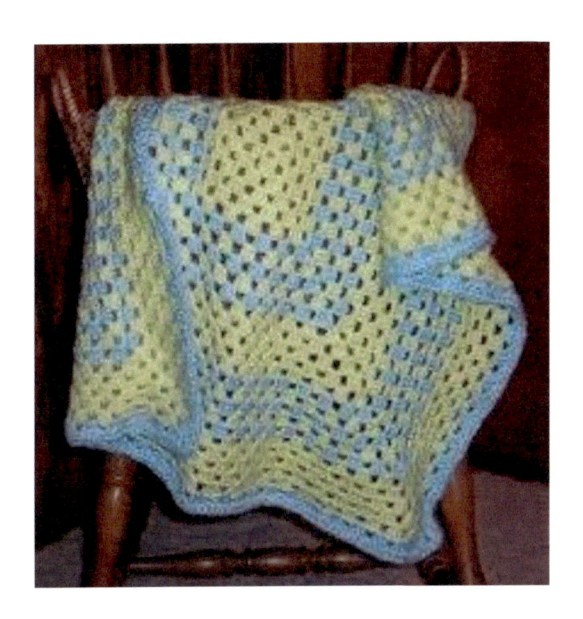

Materials:

- Approximately 20oz. for small lap blanket or 30oz. for a medium lap blanket – approximately 25% light blue and 75% light yellow
- Suggested yarn is 5oz. light weight acrylic such as Bernat Softee
- Crochet hook size 4.00mm (G/6)
- Darning needle for weaving in ends of yarn when your project is completed

Gauge:

- Granny squares can be worked in any gauge, just be sure to match your hook size to the recommendation on the label of the yarn you are using

- The first five rounds will be light yellow, followed by five rounds of alternating blue and yellow, followed by five rounds of light yellow and continuing in this manner until it finishes with two rounds of light blue
- This color pattern will continue until you are finished your project

Instructions:

Round 1:

- Begin with a slip knot
- Ch 6
- Join the last chain to the slip knot with a Sl St to make a circle
- Ch 3, then 2 DC, Ch 2 (all of the DC are made in the center of the circle)
- (3 DC, Ch 2) three times (all of the DC are made in the center of the circle)
- Sl St to join the last stitch made to the first stitch made to close the first round

Round 2:

- Ch 3, 2 DC in Ch-2 space
- Ch 2 (this makes the corner space)
- 3 DC in the same space (this sequence makes the corner and you will do the same for every corner of your project)
- Ch 2 (this is the space you will make between crochet sections throughout each granny square)
- 3 DC in next space, Ch 2, 3 DC in same space, Ch 2 (this is your second corner)

One-Day Crochet: Afghans

- 3 DC in next space, Ch 2, 3 DC in same space, Ch 2 (this is your third corner)
- 3 DC in next space, Ch 2, 3 DC in same space, Ch 2 (this is your fourth corner)
- Sl St to join the last stitch made to the third chain stitch made in this round to close the round

Round 3:

- Ch 3, 2 DC in Ch-2 space
- 3 DC in next space, Ch 2, 3 DC in same space, Ch 2 (this sequence makes the corner and you will do the same for every corner of your project)
- Ch 2 (this is the space you will make between crochet sections throughout each granny square)
- 3 DC in next space (this is not a corner) and then Ch 2
- 3 DC in next space, Ch 2, 3 DC in same space (this is your second corner)
- Ch 2 and 3 DC in next space (this is not a corner) and then Ch 2
- 3 DC in next space, Ch 2, 3 DC in same space (this is your third corner)
- Ch 2 and 3 DC in next space (this is not a corner) and then Ch 2
- 3 DC in next space, Ch 2, 3 DC in same space (this is your fourth corner)
- Ch 2 and 3 DC in next space (this is not a corner) and then Ch 2
- Sl St to join the last stitch made to the third chain stitch made in this round to close the round

Round 4 and more:

- Ch 3, 2 DC in Ch-2 space
- Ch 2 and 3 DC in the next Ch-2 space (do this for all spaces until you reach the next corner)
- Ch 2
- 3 DC in next space, Ch 2, 3 DC in same space (this sequence makes the corner and you will do the same for every corner of your project)
- Ch 2 (this is the space you will make between crochet sections throughout each granny square)
- 3 DC in next space (this is not a corner) and then Ch 2 (do this for all spaces until you reach the next corner)
- 3 DC in next space, Ch 2, 3 DC in same space, Ch 2 (this is your second corner)
- 3 DC in next space (this is not a corner) and then Ch 2 (do this for all spaces until you reach the next corner)
- 3 DC in next space, Ch 2, 3 DC in same space, Ch 2 (this is your third corner)
- 3 DC in next space (this is not a corner) and then Ch 2 (do this for all spaces until you reach the next corner)
- 3 DC in next space, Ch 2, 3 DC in same space, Ch 2 (this is your fourth corner)
- 3 DC in next space (this is not a corner) and then Ch 2 (do this for all spaces until you reach the beginning of this round)
- Sl St to join the last stitch made to the third chain stitch made in this round to close the round

- Continue to crochet rounds until your project is finished using the following color pattern:
    - 5 rounds light yellow
    - 1 round light blue
    - 1 round light yellow
    - 1 round light blue
    - 1 round light yellow
    - 1 round light blue
    - 5 rounds light yellow
    - Continue with alternating blue and yellow and 5 rounds of yellow until you are almost done
    - Finish with 2 rounds of light blue

Finish:

At the end, finish your last round by tying a knot in your yarn and cutting the yarn, leaving an approximately 6" long tail. Use your darning needle to weave the beginning tail and the ending tail and all tails from changing colors into each square.

Conclusion

Well, I hope you have been inspired to do one of the following:

- Start your first crochet project
- Finish an unfinished crochet project
- Start a new crochet project from this book
- Create a gift for someone

I hope that you feel that you are now equipped with the knowledge to start and complete a beautiful afghan. There are so many beautiful styles and colors to choose from, I am excited for you to begin your next project.

Please feel free to use the patterns in this book in various different color combinations to create your own unique masterpiece.

Happy crocheting!

Cookbooks by Barb Asselin

Click on each image to download directly from Amazon.

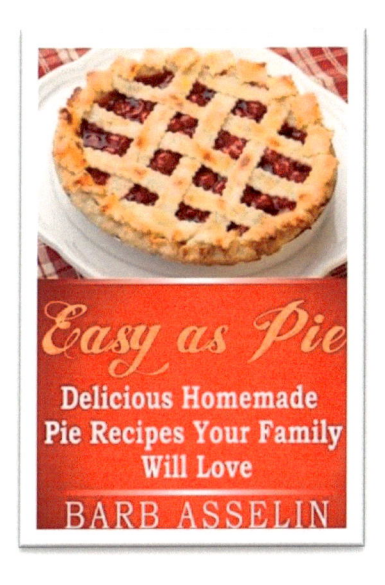

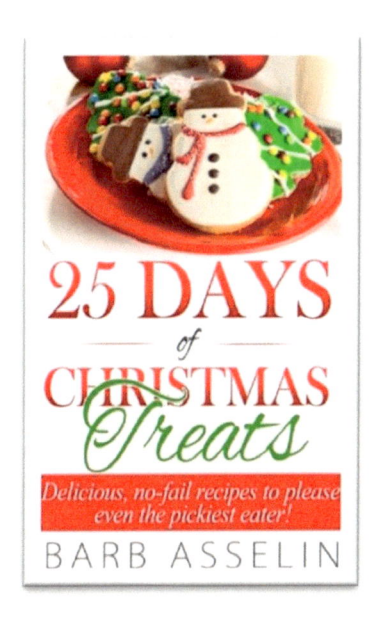

ENJOY THIS BOOK?

I see you've made it all the way to the end of my book. I'm so glad you enjoyed it enough to get all the way through! If you liked the book, would you be open to leaving me a 4 or 5 star review? You see, I'm a self-published author, and when people like you are able to give me reviews, it helps me out in a big way. You can leave a review for me at Amazon page for this book, by clicking on the picture below.

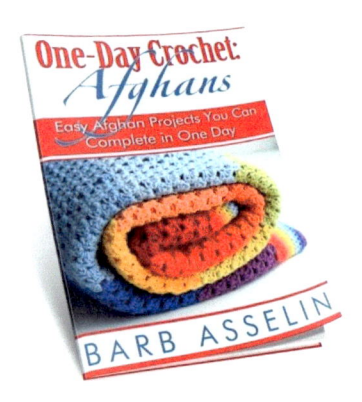

It'd really mean a lot to me.

Thank you.

Barb Asselin